GET STARTED

Before arriving, you need to plan out your day and get ready for the kids you will lead.
Use the following steps for successful preparation.

PREPARE YOUR HEART

- Read the daily Scripture passages from your Bible. Pray that God will speak to you through His Word. (See the "Checklist" on page 4.)
- Pray for the kids you will teach (page 5). Pray for yourself and the other leaders at VBS. Ask people to pray for you.

GET THE BASIC FACTS FROM YOUR VBS DIRECTOR

- Find out how long you will have Bible study each day. Look at Bible Study Schedule Options (page 4) to determine how to plan your time.
- Find out how many kids to prepare for.

PLAN

- Use these curriculum pieces:
  - This leader guide (one per teacher)
  - **VBS 2019 Grades 1–2 Bible Study Leader Pack** (005804846)—This pack includes a large banner, Bible verse poster, gameboards, other fun teaching items, and a *Music for Kids CD.* (one per classroom)
  - **VBS 2019 Field Guide: Grades 1–6** (005805594)—This fun book provides activities and tips to help kids engage in Bible study and gives them fun resources to take home at the end of the week. (one per kid)
  - **Multimedia Resources**—The 🔊 icons in this guide are to help you quickly identify audio resources.

You can find the songs on the *VBS 2019 Music for Kids CD* in the leader pack or purchase them for download from www.lifeway.com.

- Read through the daily sessions. Highlight what you plan to include. The 30-minute Bible Study Plan provides the core Bible teaching time. Additional Activity Options are included at the end of each session if your Bible study time is longer than 30 minutes.
- Make a supply list of the items you need.

GATHER AND PREPARE

- Sort and assemble items from your leader pack.
- Gather other supplies. (Some VBS directors will gather supplies for you. Check to be sure how your church does this.)

TEACH

- Relax and enjoy the chance to build relationships with your kids.
- Be flexible. Adjust your plans to make this the best experience possible for you and your kids.

CONTINUE THE CONNECTION

- Make sure your church has correct contact information for each child in your class.
- Keep the connection alive by looking for ways to stay connected with the kids you taught.

TABLE OF CONTENTS

VBS 2019 Grades 1–2 Leader Guide
Candace Powell
Content Editor
Rhonda VanCleave
Publishing Team Leader
Landry Holmes
Manager, Kids Ministry Publishing
Jana Magruder
Director, Kids Ministry
Scott Wiley
Writer
Scott teaches children at his church.

Send questions/comments to:
VBS Publishing Team Leader by email to
rhonda.vancleave@lifeway.com
Or by mail to
VBS Publishing Team Leader
1–2 Grade Leader Guide
One LifeWay Plaza
Nashville, TN 37234
or make comments on the Web at
www.lifeway.com.

Printed in the United States of America
© Copyright 2018 LifeWay Press

We believe that the Bible has God for its author;
salvation for its end; and truth, without any mixture
of error, for its matter and that all Scripture is totally
true and trustworthy. To review LifeWay's doctrinal
guideline, please visit
www.lifeway.com/doctrinalguideline.

Unless otherwise indicated, all Scripture
quotations are taken from the Christian Standard
Bible®, Copyright 2017 by Holman Bible Publishers.
Used by permission.

VBS SCRIPTURE

But these are written so that you may believe that Jesus is the Messiah, the Son of God, and that by believing you may have life in his name. *John 20:31*

But these are written, that ye might believe that Jesus is the Christ, the Son of God; and that believing ye might have life through his name. *John 20:31 (KJV)*

VBS MOTTO: ZOOM IN! FOCUS ON JESUS!

Gas up the all-terrain vehicle and head out on a wilderness adventure like no other. Get up close and personal with elephants and egrets, polar bears and penguins, cockatoos and crocodiles, and so much more! Grab your camera and zoom in on these animals in their natural habitats. Maybe you can even snag a snapshot or two. This summer kids will focus in on some amazing, real-life encounters with Jesus. Each encounter is like a snapshot—a specific moment in time captured on the pages of Scripture. Through VBS, kids will discover that each snapshot of Jesus is an opportunity to respond to the gospel. And when put together, these isolated encounters clearly reveal the most amazing truth of all—Jesus Christ is the Messiah, the Son of God, and by believing we can have life in His name. Are you ready for an up close and personal encounter with Jesus? The adventure of a lifetime awaits!

Day 1 Encounter in the Temple—When Jesus was 12 years old, He traveled with His family to Jerusalem for the Passover Festival. After the celebration Mary and Joseph headed back to Nazareth. After traveling a full day they realized Jesus was not with them. They hurried back to Jerusalem and finally, on the third day, Mary and Joseph found Jesus in the temple. Jesus was listening to the teachers and asking questions. Everyone was amazed at how much Jesus understood at such a young age. (Luke 2:41-52)

Day 2 Encounter at the River—John helped people get ready for Jesus, God's promised Messiah. John told people to repent of their sins and be baptized. One day Jesus came to the river and John told the people Jesus was the One he had been speaking about. Jesus asked John to baptize Him to follow God's plan. After Jesus was baptized, an amazing thing happened. The Holy Spirit appeared to Jesus in the form of a dove and God declared that Jesus is indeed His Son! (Matthew 3:1-17)

Day 3 Encounter on the Water—After a long day teaching near the Sea of Galilee, Jesus sent the disciples ahead of Him in a boat. Late at night there was a storm and the waves beat against the boat. The disciples saw Jesus walking to them on top of the water, and they were frightened. After Jesus identified Himself, Peter asked to come to Him on the water. Jesus said, "Come." As Peter walked to Jesus, he became afraid and began to sink. Peter called out for Jesus to save him. Jesus reached out, caught hold of Peter, and got back in the boat with him. The wind immediately stopped, and the disciples proclaimed that Jesus really is the Son of God! (Matthew 14:22-33)

Day 4 Encounter at the Tomb—On the third day after Jesus had died on a cross and been buried, Mary Magdalene went to the tomb. As she approached the tomb, she saw that the stone had been rolled away. Mary went and told Peter and John who came to see for themselves. After Peter and John left, Mary looked into the tomb. She saw two angels. They asked why she was crying. A man standing nearby asked who she was looking for. Mary thought the man was the gardener, but when He said her name she recognized His voice. It was Jesus! He sent Mary to share the amazing news with His disciples. Jesus is alive! (John 20:1-18)

Day 5 Encounter on the Road—Two men were walking toward the village of Emmaus talking about everything that had happened during the last week. Jesus joined them, but they did not recognize Him. The men began explaining everything that had happened to Jesus and that He was a great Prophet. Jesus began telling them about Himself using Scripture to explain why all the things had happened. When they arrived in Emmaus, Jesus stayed to eat with them. As Jesus tore the bread and gave pieces to the men, they recognized Him. Jesus immediately disappeared from their sight. The men returned to Jerusalem and told the disciples about their amazing encounter with the risen Jesus. (Luke 24:13-35)

Christ Connection: The Bible tells us what is true about God and about ourselves. Jesus is the Messiah, the Son of God. When we trust in Jesus as Savior and Lord, He forgives our sin and gives us eternal life.

LOBL: (Jesus) Jesus was sent to be my Savior.

CHECKLIST

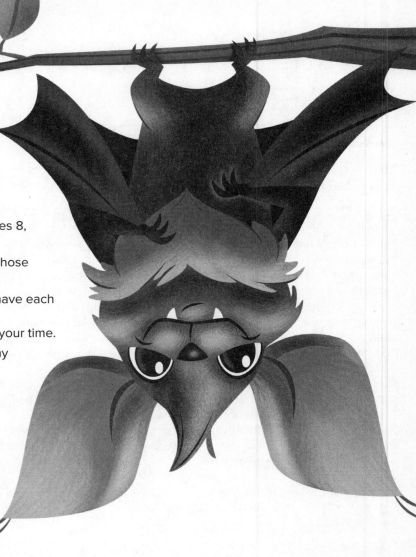

- Read the Bible content for all five days.
  - Day 1—Luke 2:41-52
  - Day 2—Matthew 3:1-17
  - Day 3—Matthew 14:22-33
  - Day 4—John 20:1-18
  - Day 5—Luke 24:13-35
- Read the "Leader Devotions" for each session (pages 8, 15, 22, 29, 36).
- Pray for yourself, other VBS leaders, and the kids whose lives you will touch.
- Find out from your VBS director how long you will have each day for Bible study. Look at the Bible Study Schedule Options below to determine how to plan your time.
- Read through each day's session. Make notes of any changes or adjustments.
- Gather supplies and prepare to teach.

BIBLE STUDY SCHEDULE OPTIONS

- My director has told me that I will have:
  - 30 minutes for Bible Study—Use the 30-minute Bible Study Plan as written for each session. You will not need the Additional Activity Options unless you choose to substitute one of the Additional Activities for an activity in the 30-minute plan.
  - 40 or more minutes for Bible Study—Use the 30-minute Bible Study Plan. Then, select activities from the Additional Activity Options found at the end of each session to extend your time as needed.
  - Two Bible Study Times (opening and closing Bible study sessions)—Use the 30-minute Bible Study Plan during the opening session. Add Additional Activity Options as needed for an opening session of more than 30 minutes. Use any of the remaining Additional Activity Options for the closing Bible study time.

CHARACTERISTICS OF FIRST AND SECOND GRADERS

During VBS, kids will have the opportunity to learn that a personal relationship with Jesus Christ is crucial. To help you lead kids of this age to begin and grow their relationship with Jesus, here are a few tips to keep in mind.

1st and 2nd graders shift quickly from one activity to the next and are extremely active. They benefit from a variety of high, moderate, and low energy activities. They use their entire bodies to learn. They benefit from learning experiences that incorporate all senses.

1st and 2nd graders love discovering things and having opportunities to be creative. They benefit from activities like solving simple codes, playing games, or retelling the Bible story through drama.

1st and 2nd graders are learning to view Jesus as a friend and are beginning to feel the need to trust Jesus as Savior. They benefit from teachers who lovingly share information about what becoming a Christian means without putting pressure on them to make an immediate decision. Children should be reassured that it's OK if they don't feel God's Holy Spirit leading them to trust Jesus right now.

1st and 2nd graders are limited in their ability to think abstractly. They benefit from teachers who explain things clearly in simple terms without the use of abstract object lessons or analogies. They understand better when directions are short and simple.

1st and 2nd graders are focused on their own needs and moving toward independence. They benefit from simple rules and routines that are consistent. However, they like opportunities to make simple choices.

1st and 2nd graders are sensitive and desire approval. They can experience sudden mood swings. They benefit from positive words and encouraging facial expressions. They respond to teachers who listen to them and are patient with them during trying times.

DECORATING THE WATERING HOLE

The Watering Hole is an oasis where animals come together to share a cool, refreshing drink of water. What better place to serve as the backdrop for Bible study! Use the following ideas to jump start your creativity in creating an oasis for children to gather:

- Hang the *VBS 2019 Supersized Backdrop* (005809187) on the focal wall.
- Place artificial rocks and greenery in front of the backdrop.
- Cover the floor with a blue tarp or flat sheet to resemble water.
- Bunch up natural-colored canvas tarps or flat sheets around the edges of the blue tarp to create a sandy-colored ground surrounding the watering hole.
- Place the *VBS 2019 Jumbo Inflatable Elephant* (005810044) near the water's edge. Add other large stuffed animals, cardboard cutouts, or 3-D animals (see *VBS 2019 Decorating Made Easy* [005804864] for instructions).
- As you determine how to set up your Bible study, you may want to select one wall as your focal wall to display teaching items from the *VBS 2019 Grades 1–2 Bible Study Leader Pack* (005804846). Other areas of the room can include items that might be found at a watering hole. Keeping the focal wall simple with teaching items only will eliminate distractions while teaching biblical truths.
- Display the "Watering Hole Banner" (pack item 1) throughout the week and add the "Daily Snapshots" (pack item 2) each day.
- Prepare to change out the remaining pack items as they are called for each day.

Item 1

FUN OPTIONS

❏ Display a *VBS 2019 Bible Study Location Sign* (005810042) outside the room. Add punch outs from the *VBS 2019 Wall Art* (005810040) around the signs.

❏ Line the *VBS 2019 Removable Paw Prints* (005809169) on the floor outside the door to lead kids into the room. Or use them to mark a spot on the floor for each child to sit or stand upon after entering the room.

❏ Hang a *VBS 2019 Visual Pack* (005810041) poster on the wall.

❏ Use small containers or *VBS 2019 Cups* (005809129) to hold pens and supplies for each class.

❏ See *VBS 2019 Decorating Made Easy* (005804864) for additional decorating ideas.

Supersized Backdrop (005809187)

Removable Paw Prints (005809169)

Super Duper Sized Backdrop (005810039)

DAY 1

ENCOUNTER IN THE TEMPLE

BIBLE STORY

Encounter in the Temple (Luke 2:41-52)

BIBLE VERSE

But these are written so that you may believe that Jesus is the Messiah, the Son of God, and that by believing you may have life in his name. *John 20:31*

But these are written, that ye might believe that Jesus is the Christ, the Son of God; and that believing ye might have life through his name. *John 20:31* (KJV)

TODAY'S POINT

Jesus knew why He came.

LEADER DEVOTIONS

Our family recently went on a trip to the mountains—three generations of wild and crazy fun. I was still recovering from a recent surgery, so I opted to enjoy the beauty from my front porch rocking chair while the rest went for a hike in the woods. As they returned, the youngest came racing up to me, "Guess what we saw? It was an elk! And it was RIGHT THERE!" In a few moments the rest had gathered and young and old alike were telling of that moment with childlike enthusiasm. "I wish you could have been there!" The hike had taken a couple of hours, but those few unexpected moments were what changed a fun but ordinary day into a never-to-be-forgotten moment.

During VBS this week, you will be sharing stories that appear to be simple words printed on the pages of your Bible. They will be brief moments to describe. But you have the opportunity to share how these snapshots, frozen on the pages of Scripture, are never-to-be-forgotten moments ordained by God. Each one gives us a glimpse into His amazing gift, His Son Jesus, who is the Savior of the world.

Today's passage chronicles the first recorded words of Jesus. A lot of unanswered questions exist between the few tidbits we know of Jesus' birth and early childhood and the twelve-year-old in today's story. Luke, the writer of this Gospel, was obviously enthralled by the details of Jesus' life. In fact, the word translated "amazed" or "astounded" is found thirteen times in the Book of Luke. It is also interesting to note that many scholars believe Mary, Jesus' mother, was one of Luke's sources of information. As a physician and acquaintance of Mary, it is not surprising that Luke's Gospel includes some of the details of Jesus' early life.

Traveling to Jerusalem for the Passover Festival was an annual custom. The distance from Nazareth to Jerusalem was about seventy miles. The average distance traveled per day may have been between twenty and twenty-five miles. So, this journey would have taken three or four days. The festival lasted a week, and then the return journey began. Families and friends generally traveled together for companionship as well as safety. As a twelve-year-old, Jesus was less than a year away from being considered an adult Jewish male. Under these circumstances it was probably easy to assume that Jesus was somewhere in the group of travelers. How Jesus ended up talking with the teachers at the temple or how long He had been there is unclear. However we do know that, at day's end, His absence was discovered.

The Bible doesn't tell us what Mary and Joseph said or thought as they retraced a day's worth of travel and began the search through the large city. As a parent, I can only imagine the various waves of emotion that must have colored those hours. We see a hint of it in Mary's first words to Jesus, "Son, why have you treated us like this? Your father and I have been anxiously searching for you."

Jesus answered with, "Why were you searching?" At this point Mary and Joseph seemed to be struggling with understanding the full meaning of who their Son was. However, by age twelve, Jesus indicated full awareness. He was in "His Father's house." This was not a put down to Joseph who had the earthly responsibility of serving as father. Jesus was acknowledging who He is. He is the Son of God.

Luke (most likely a Gentile) used carefully investigated facts presented in an orderly sequence to his friend, Theophilus, to shore up his friend's belief with certainty (Luke 1:1-4). May Luke's words do the same for us over two thousand years later. Pray that the Holy Spirit will shine a light on your path as you read God's Word and may you encounter Jesus like never before.

PERSONAL FOCUS

- Read John 6:38 (today's bonus verse). What truths about Jesus do you find in this verse?
- As you read today's Bible passage what "snapshot" stood out to you? What was intriguing about it?
- Before you can teach kids about Jesus, it is important that you have had your own personal encounter with the Savior. How would you describe your relationship with Jesus to someone else?

TEACH THE BIBLE STUDY (30 MINUTES)

START IT PREP
- ❑ Leader pack items 1, 3

START IT (5 MINUTES)

1. Give each kid one of the "Animal Pictures" (pack item 3), or group the kids into pairs and give each pair an animal picture. Say: "Okay, animals, let's group up together. Group up by number of legs—4, 2, 0. Go!" If necessary, indicate where animals with four legs should group, where two legs should group, and so forth. After they have grouped up, call a different way to group (can fly/cannot fly; can swim/cannot swim; live on water/land; live in hot/temperate/cold climates; etc). Collect pictures.

2. Welcome kids to the Watering Hole. Point to the "Watering Hole Banner" (pack item 1). Tell kids that at the Watering Hole they may encounter all kinds of animals. Every animal must take in water at some time and will venture to the watering hole to get what they need. Tell kids that they will be having all kinds of unexpected encounters this week—encounters with different animals and encounters with Jesus.

LEARN IT PREP
- ❑ Leader pack items 4, 5, 7, and 8 or 9
- ❑ Tape the "Story Stops" (pack item 5) in different locations around the room

LEARN IT (15 MINUTES)

1. Call attention to the "Story Stops" (pack item 5) around the room. Gather the kids with you to stand near the "Nazareth" sign. Tell the kids that today's story takes place when Jesus was 12 years old; Jesus and His family lived in Nazareth. Tell kids to be ready to move during the Bible story.

2. Open the Bible to Luke 2:41-52. Tell the Bible story in your own words. Move to the different story stops as indicated during the story. Make sure kids move with you and stay engaged as you tell the Bible story.

ITEM 4

ENCOUNTER IN THE TEMPLE

(Nazareth) When Jesus was 12 years old, He traveled with His family to Jerusalem for the Passover Festival. Passover was a time to celebrate and remember when God rescued His people from slavery in Egypt.

(Temple) They went to the temple and celebrated. After the celebration was over, Mary and Joseph began the trip back to Nazareth with a large group of family and friends.

(Traveling Group) They did not notice that Jesus was not with them. They thought He was with the others who were traveling back together. But Jesus was not with the group. He was still in Jerusalem.

(Oasis) Mary, Joseph, and the other travelers had been walking for an entire day when they realized Jesus was missing. They looked among their family and friends, but they could not find Him.

(Jerusalem) So Mary and Joseph went back to Jerusalem to look for Jesus. They searched everywhere, but could not find Him.

(Temple) Finally, on the third day, they found Jesus in the temple. He was sitting with the teachers, listening to them and asking questions.

The teachers were amazed at how much Jesus understood. They had spent their entire lives studying the Scriptures, but Jesus was just a boy. How could He already know so much and ask such good questions?

When Jesus' parents saw Him, they were surprised. Mary said, "We've been looking everywhere for You!"

"Why were you looking for Me?" Jesus asked. "Didn't you know I would be in my Father's house?" Jesus knew that He was God's Son. But Mary and Joseph did not understand what Jesus was telling them.

(Nazareth) Jesus went back to Nazareth with His parents and was always obedient to them. Jesus continued to grow. He grew taller and wiser as He became a man. God was pleased with Him, and so were people who knew Him.

Luke 2:41-52

3. Show the "Day 1 Bible Story Picture" (pack item 4). Ask kids to tell what they remember about the things Jesus said. Say: "Jesus knew why He came. He knew that He is God's Son."

4. Display the "Verse Map" (pack item 7). Mix the "Verse Strips" (pack item 8 or 9) and read the phrases, one at a time, to the kids. Lead kids to attach the strips to the map in order. (Use the icons to help place the strips.) Read the verse together.

5. Lead kids to find John 20:31 in Bibles (individually or in pairs). Point out that the part of the verse that says "these are written" refers to the things in the Bible that are written about Jesus.

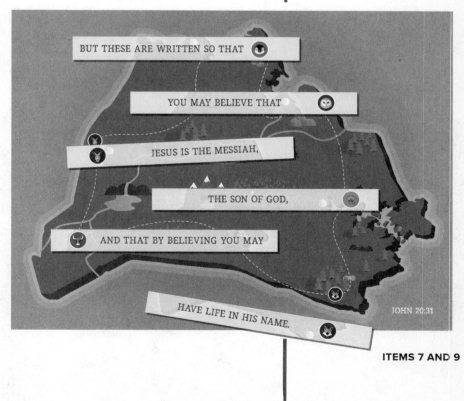

BUT THESE ARE WRITTEN SO THAT

YOU MAY BELIEVE THAT

JESUS IS THE MESSIAH,

THE SON OF GOD,

AND THAT BY BELIEVING YOU MAY

HAVE LIFE IN HIS NAME.

JOHN 20:31

ITEMS 7 AND 9

TEACH THE BIBLE STUDY (30 MINUTES)

LIVE IT PREP
- ❏ Leader pack items 1, 2
- ❏ *VBS 2019 Field Guides: Grades 1–6* (1 per kid)
- ❏ Large piece of paper

LIVE IT (8 MINUTES)

1. Attach "Daily Snapshot 1" (pack item 2) to the "Watering Hole Banner" (pack item 1). Say: "Jesus knew why He came. Because we have the Bible, we can know why Jesus came, too. Jesus is the Savior. We will learn more about Jesus this week."

2. Lead kids to tell what they know about Jesus and tell why they think He came. Write down their ideas on the large piece of paper. Say: "We will keep this chart all week. We will decide if we need to add or change anything as we learn more about Jesus in VBS."

3. Distribute the Field Guides and pencils. Tell kids to find "Track It Down" (page 3). Read the activity and tell kids to draw something they might see to show that an animal was nearby. Say that we have evidence that Jesus knew why He came because we read it in the Bible.

FINISH IT PREP
- ❏ *VBS 2019 Field Guides: Grades 1–6* (1 per kid)
- ❏ *VBS 2019 Daily Verse Tags* (005809144)

FINISH IT (2 MINUTES)

1. Call attention to "Up Close and Personal" (page 3). Read the question. Tell kids they can search for more evidence about Jesus in the Bible.

2. If you have the Daily Verse Tags, distribute the Day 1 tags and encourage kids to look up the verse on their tag.

3. Pray. Thank God for Jesus' coming and doing God's will.

GROWTH CHART

(APPLICATION ACTIVITY—10 MINUTES)

PREP

❏ Leader pack item 12

1. Comment that animals in the wild grow as God designed for them to grow. They live in their habitats and do things as God created them to do.

2. Remind kids that Jesus was 12 years old in today's Bible story. Jesus continued to grow into a man.

3. Group kids into pairs. Distribute copies of "Jesus Grew" (pack item 12), and give each pair a Bible. Tell kids to locate Luke 2:52 and write it in the space on their pages. Note that Jesus grew in four ways—wisdom, stature, in favor with God, and in favor with people/man. Lead pairs to make matches on the page. Briefly talk about what each of these mean.

4. Tell kids that they are growing in similar ways that Jesus grew. Tell pairs to talk about ways that children grow today in the four different ways. Lead kids to write or draw at least one way they are growing like Jesus grew.

5. Ask kids to think about why Jesus came. Kids can jot down their thoughts on the page. Lead pairs to open the Bible to John 20:31. Read the verse together. Say: "Jesus came to save us."

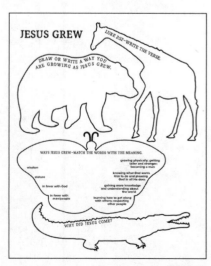

ITEM 12

ANIMAL CAMOUFLAGE

(Application Activity—10 minutes)

PREP

❏ Leader pack item 3

❏ Paper

❏ Crayons

1. Tell kids that God created animals to live and survive in their different habitats. Choose an "Animal Picture" (pack item 3) and show the kids. Ask them to tell what traits that animal has that help it survive. Repeat with a couple of other animals.

2. Group kids into groups of 2–4. Give each group paper and crayons. Tell the kids they are going to "design" their own animal. The animal must be able to move quickly and to blend into its surroundings. Tell kids to think about where their animal lives and what it would look like. After a few minutes, call the kids back together. Groups can quickly show their animals and talk about why the animals look as they do.

3. Tell kids that God made each of them for a purpose—to glorify Him. Say that God gives each person different talents and abilities to use to glorify God. Tell kids to think of things they can do well. Say: "Whatever your talents and abilities, whatever you like to do, God wants you to use that to glorify and praise Him."

4. Say that Jesus had a purpose when He came to earth. Open the Bible to John 6:38 and read the bonus verse for today. Say: "Jesus knew why He came. He came to do God's will."

5. Repeat the point with kids: "Jesus knew why He came."

ITEM 3

TIGER TAILS

(Bible Skills Activity—10 minutes)

PREP

- ❏ Leader pack item 6
- ❏ Wide craft sticks
- ❏ Orange markers
- ❏ Narrow black ribbon or black paper
- ❏ Scissors
- ❏ Glue

1. Talk about the two parts of the Bible. Explain that the Bible has an Old Testament and a New Testament. Say that the Old Testament, the first part of the Bible, tells about God and His people before Jesus was born. The New Testament, the second part of the Bible, tells about Jesus' birth and life and what happened with the church after Jesus returned to heaven.

2. Ask: "Which part of the Bible has today's story in it? Remember that we heard about something that happened when Jesus was a boy." *(New Testament)*

3. Tell kids that they can learn how to find the New Testament in the Bible. Demonstrate as you explain. Open the Bible to the middle of the Bible. Then open the second half of the Bible to the middle. When you do this, you should be in the New Testament or close to it.

4. Lead kids to practice this method of finding the New Testament. Ask someone to read the name of the Bible book in an open Bible. Note if it is in the New Testament or close to it.

5. Tell kids that they can make a tiger tail Bible marker to place at the New Testament in their own Bibles. Distribute supplies. Lead kids to color the craft sticks with the orange markers. When they finish, they can cut short lengths of ribbon or short strips of paper to glue across the craft stick to make tiger stripes.

6. Tell kids that the VBS verse is also in the New Testament. Display the "John 20:31 Poster" (pack item 6). Read the verse together. Tell kids that they can read in the New Testament to learn more about Jesus, God's Son.

RABBIT RUN

(Bonus Verse Activity—10 minutes)

PREP

- ❏ Leader pack item 13
- ❏ Self-stick notes or note cards (one color per team)

1. Print the words of the verse on notes or note cards, one or two words per card. Make a set of words for each team. Mix the words and stick them all around the space.

2. Show the "John 6:38 Poster" (pack item 13). Read the verse together. Say: "These are words that Jesus said. Jesus knew why He came. He came to do God's will."

3. Group the kids into teams; assign one color note to each team. Tell kids that they will need to take turns getting a word and bringing it back to the team. The team can work together to put the words in order. Tell teams that this is "Rabbit Run." Each team member will need to hold hands up against his head to resemble rabbit ears. He will hop to get a word and return to the team.

4. Prepare the first players from each team and tell them to go. Encourage teams to continue to retrieve words and work to put the verse in order. When a team has completed the verse, lead team members to shout, "In the wild!"

5. Say the verse together again.

6. As time permits, reset and play again. Tell teams to scatter their words all over the room. Then switch colors among teams or remix teams and play again.

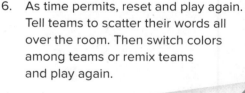

DAY 2

ENCOUNTER AT THE RIVER

BIBLE STORY

Encounter at the River (Matthew 3:1-17)

BIBLE VERSE

But these are written so that you may believe that Jesus is the Messiah, the Son of God, and that by believing you may have life in his name. *John 20:31*

But these are written, that ye might believe that Jesus is the Christ, the Son of God; and that believing ye might have life through his name. *John 20:31* (KJV)

TODAY'S POINT

Jesus is the Son of God.

LEADER DEVOTION

As you flip through dozens of snapshots, all evidence of amazing moments and fond memories, do you ever find one that causes you to stop and gaze in amazement? Then, you begin to envision all the fabulous ways to display it! Today's Scripture snapshot is one that is worth enlarging, mounting, and hanging! In this one frozen-in-time moment we see the obedience of the Son, the blessing of the Spirit, and the declaration of the Father—God in three persons—Blessed Trinity.

Matthew included the details of Jesus' baptism in his Gospel as did Mark and Luke. All three acknowledge that John the baptizer was the one Isaiah had prophesied about who would herald the coming Messiah (Isaiah 40:3). You don't have to dig very deep in the New Testament to know for certain that John the baptizer was sent as the forerunner of Jesus. Jesus Himself called John the greatest of all prophets (Matthew 11:9-13).

People from Jerusalem, all around Judea, and the vicinity of the Jordan came to the wilderness where John had been preaching. His message convicted those who heard and many confessed their sins. Baptism was symbolic, even then, of changing one's mind and going a new direction.

Many people feel puzzled about why Jesus came to be baptized. John was preaching a message of repentance symbolized by the rite of baptism. Since Jesus was "the one who did not know sin" (2 Corinthians 5:21) why would He place Himself in such an act of submission? In one respect, this action on Jesus' part gave validity to John's message and ministry. But, the prevailing reason was Jesus was being obedient to the Father. This simple act was symbolic of an entire life that was obedient— obedient even unto death (Philippians 2:8). No step of God's plan could be skipped if Jesus was to fulfill all He came to do.

John, understandably, resisted at first. But Jesus explained that they must do this to "fulfill all righteousness."

(v. 15) So, John complied. What happened next is that picture-perfect moment—the obedience of the Son, the presence of the Spirit, and the affirmation of the Father. For John the Baptist, this visible presence of the Spirit was confirmation of a promise he had received that Jesus was indeed the Son of God (John 1:32-34).

Twice in the Book of Matthew, God spoke from heaven declaring that Jesus is His Son. We read about it here and later at the transfiguration (Matthew 17:5). Many commentaries explain that God's declaration combines phrases from Psalms and Isaiah. The first portion echoes Psalm 2:7, which was used at the coronation of Israel's kings. The second portion alludes to Isaiah 42:1, declaring Jesus to be the Servant promised. Jesus is the King of kings and the Suffering Servant who became our Savior.

Who heard the voice of God? The Scripture is unclear. Many believe those present heard. Either way, Matthew was confident enough to describe it here and John the Baptist described the event later in the Gospel of John (John 1:32-34). This amazing encounter was the official inauguration of the ministry phase of Jesus' life. Jesus stepped out of the waters of the Jordan on a journey that would end in three short years at the cross.

PERSONAL FOCUS

- Read John 1:34 (today's bonus verse). What were some encounters that helped John declare this with certainty?

- What are experiences that have helped you know for certain that Jesus is the Son of God?

- Take a few moments to pray for kids who will attend your class. Pray that they will come to truly know that Jesus is God's Son and that He loves them.

START IT (4 MINUTES)

1. Welcome kids to Bible study at VBS. Ask kids to tell about a time they saw an animal in the wild or an unexpected animal up close *(at the zoo, etc.)*.

2. Tell kids that animals are hiding around the Watering Hole. "Spy" one of the hidden animals on the "Watering Hole Banner" (pack item 1) and tell kids what you spy. Take turns looking on the banner to find the hidden animal. Repeat as time allows.

3. Call attention to yesterday's point (pack item 2) and say it together. Tell kids they will discover more about Jesus today.

4. Ask for volunteers to pray. Ask them to pray and ask God to help everyone learn more about encounters that people had with Jesus.

LEARN IT (12 MINUTES)

1. Tell kids: "Today we were spying animals around the watering hole. In our Bible story, people were not gathered at a watering hole, but at a river. A man spied someone at the river."

2. Open the Bible to Matthew 3:1-17. Show the "Day 2 Bible Story Picture" (pack item 14). Tell the Bible story in your own words. Change the tone of your voice as you tell the story, generating more interest.

ENCOUNTER AT THE RIVER

God gave John a special job even before John was born. John was going to help people get ready for Jesus, God's promised Messiah. Hundreds of years before John was born, the prophet Isaiah wrote that there would be a voice crying out in the wilderness saying, "Prepare the way for the Lord." John was that person. When John grew up, he went to the desert and people from all over Judea came to hear him. But he explained to people: "There is someone coming who is more powerful and greater than I." Of course John was speaking about Jesus, but the people didn't know it yet.

As John taught about Jesus, the people were sorry for the wrong things they had done. They repented to God of their sins and decided to do what God wanted them to do. They wanted to please God. John began baptizing people in the Jordan River.

By this time, Jesus was an adult. One day He came to the river where John was teaching and baptizing people. When John saw Jesus he said to everyone, "This is the One I told you about! Jesus is the One who takes away the sin of the world!"

Jesus asked John to baptize Him. But John didn't think he was worthy to baptize Jesus. John only baptized sinners, and Jesus had never sinned. But Jesus insisted. He told John, "Allow Me to be baptized. God says this is right." John agreed and baptized Jesus.

START IT PREP
☐ Leader pack items 1, 2

LEARN IT PREP
☐ Leader pack items 6, 8 or 9, 10, 14, 15
☐ Self-stick notes
☐ Animal stickers
☐ Place animal stickers on the self-stick notes, one animal per note. On the back of each note (on the sticky side), print (small size) one of these values: +3, +2, +1, -1, -2, -3. Stick the notes on a wall. Label the two sides of the "Anaconda Chart" (pack item 15) with sticky notes: Team 1 and Team 2.

ITEM 14

ITEM 12

> When Jesus came up out of the water, the heavens opened up and He saw the Holy Spirit coming down from heaven like a dove. God's voice said, "This is My Son. I love Him, and I am very pleased with Him." What an amazing thing to hear God's own voice declaring that Jesus is His Son!
>
> *Matthew 3:1-17*

3. Group the kids into two teams. Tell teams you will play "Capture the Animal." Teams can answer questions about the Bible story. When a team answers a question correctly, they can choose which animal to capture. Alternate asking teams to respond to questions about the story. Use the "Review Questions" (pack item 10) or other questions about the story. When a team answers correctly and chooses an animal, move that animal to the appropriate side of the "Anaconda Chart" (pack item 15), (but do not show the back of the note). After all questions have been answered, flip over the notes and total the score, adding or subtracting points as designated. The team with the higher score wins.

4. Open the Bible to John 20:31 and read the verse to kids. Hand out the "Verse Strips" (pack item 8 or 9). Lead those kids to stand in front of the group and hold their strips. Read the strips. Lead the group to place the strips in order. Group the kids into six groups. Assign a group to read each strip. Lead the groups to say their phrases in order.

LIVE IT (9 MINUTES)

1. Distribute the learner guides and pencils. Lead kids to find "Spot It!" (page 5) and look for the hidden words. Identify which words are from the Bible verse.

2. Attach "Daily Snapshot 2" (pack item 2) to the "Watering Hole Banner" (pack item 1). Say: "Jesus is the Son of God. How did the people in today's Bible story learn that Jesus is the Son of God? *(heard God's voice say it)* How do we know that Jesus is the Son of God?" *(the Bible tells us)*

3. Review the statements listed about Jesus from your homemade chart. Determine with the kids if any statement needs to be changed or deleted. Ask: "What statements about Jesus should we add?" Add today's point if that statement isn't already on the chart. Children may want to add the other names of Jesus they found hidden in "Spot It."

LIVE IT PREP
- ☐ Leader pack items 1, 2
- ☐ *VBS 2019 Field Guides: Grades 1–6* (1 per kid)
- ☐ Homemade Jesus chart from Day 1

FINISH IT (5 MINUTES)

1. Call attention to "Up Close and Personal" (page 5) in the Field Guide. Say: "Jesus said other things about Himself. These Bible verses tell things that Jesus said. Today read at least one of these verses and discover something that Jesus said."

2. Play the song "Worthy Of All Praise"  (track 5). Tell kids to listen for something about Jesus in the song.

3. If you have the Daily Verse Tags, distribute the Day 2 tags and encourage kids to look up the verse on their tag.

4. Pray, thanking God for giving us His Son.

FINISH IT PREP
- ❏ *VBS 2019 Field Guides: Grades 1–6* (1 per kid)
- ❏ *VBS 2019 Daily Verse Tags* (005809144)
- ❏ *Music for Kids CD*
  - "Worthy of All Praise" (track 5)

MULTIMEDIA KEY
🔊 Audio
See page 1 for more information.

ADDITIONAL ACTIVITY OPTIONS

ANIMAL TAGS
(Application Activity—10 minutes)

PREP

- ❏ Circle key tags with split rings
- ❏ Scissors
- ❏ Colored cardstock
- ❏ Glue
- ❏ Gel pens
- ❏ ***Note:*** Instead of circle key tags, cut cardstock into 1¼ inch circles and punch holes in the circles; purchase split rings or binder rings.

1. Say Today's Point with kids. Ask kids to tell how the people in the Bible story knew that Jesus is God's Son *(John told them; God said so)*. Ask kids to tell how people today learn that Jesus is God's Son *(Read in the Bible; other people tell them)*.

2. Say: "We can help others know that Jesus is God's Son." Show kids the materials and tell them they can make tags for their backpacks that tell about Jesus.

3. Tell kids to print Today's Point on one side of their tags. They can decorate the other side of the tags to look like animals. They may want to draw markings or faces on the circles. They can cut out ears or legs to glue to their tags.

PICTURE THIS
(Application Activity—10 minutes)

PREP

- ❏ Leader pack items 3, 14
- ❏ Photograph of the baptistry or place where people are baptized in your church

1. Lay the "Animal Pictures" (pack item 3) in front of the kids. Say: "Sometimes we use animals as pictures or symbols of other things. Look at these animals. Which animal would you use to be a picture or symbol of strength?" Allow 1–2 kids to respond, giving their reasoning. Ask for pictures or symbols of speed, intelligence, clumsiness, or slowness.

2. Display the "Day 2 Bible Story Picture" (pack item 14). Say: "Pictures or symbols help us understand things that may be hard to explain. Today in the Bible story, something happened to Jesus. What was it?" *(He was baptized.)*

3. Ask: "How is someone baptized?" Listen as the kids tell their ideas. Explain that being baptized is placing a person under the water and then bringing him back up.

4. Say: "People are baptized when they become Christians. Baptism does not make a person a Christian. Baptism does not save a person. Baptism is a picture or symbol that someone has trusted Jesus as Savior. People who are baptized are following Jesus' example."

5. Show the photograph of where people are baptized in your church. Talk about times the children have seen someone baptized or been baptized themselves. Answer questions that children may have about baptism.

6. Option: Invite the pastor or someone from the baptismal committee to explain how your church does baptisms (show the robe, etc.).

FLIPPER SLAP
(Bible Skills Activity—10 minutes)

PREP
- ❏ Leader pack item 16
- ❏ 2 large gray oven mitts
- ❏ For this game, you will need the Gospel book cards and 8–10 other Bible book cards from the "New Testament Cards" (pack item 16).

1. Tell kids that the books in the Bible that tell about Jesus' life are called the Gospels. Review which books are the Gospels—Matthew, Mark, Luke, John.
2. Group the kids into two teams. Lead each team to stand on either side of the room. Mix and scatter the Bible book cards, faceup, on the floor between the teams.
3. Give the first player on each team an oven mitt to wear. Say: "You are seals and these are your flippers. I will call out either Gospel or Not Gospel. You will slap (with your flipper) and call out a Bible book that matches what I say."
4. Call out: "Gospel!" Both kids should slap one of the Gospel books and call out what they slap.
5. Lead players to hand off the flipper to the next player on the team. Call out, "Gospel," or "Not Gospel." Continue until all players have a turn.
6. Say: "We know that Jesus is God's Son by reading the Gospels and learning what He did. Say the Gospels with me, 'Matthew! Mark! Luke! John!'"

GOSPELS	LUKE	FIRST AND SECOND THESSALONIANS
HISTORY	JOHN	FIRST AND SECOND TIMOTHY
PAUL'S LETTERS	JOHN	TITUS
GENERAL LETTERS	ACTS	PHILEMON
PROPHECY	ROMANS	HEBREWS
MATTHEW	FIRST AND SECOND CORINTHIANS	JAMES
MATTHEW	GALATIANS	FIRST AND SECOND PETER
MARK	EPHESIANS	FIRST, SECOND, AND THIRD JOHN
MARK	PHILIPPIANS	JUDE
LUKE	COLOSSIANS	REVELATION

ITEM 16

CROC ATTACK
(Bonus Verse Activity—10 minutes)

PREP
- ❏ Leader pack item 17
- ❏ Clothespins (green if available)
- ❏ Timer
- ❏ Mark two eyes on the end of the clothespins so that they resemble crocodiles. Print a word of John 1:34 on each clothespin. To make the game more challenging, add a few random words to clothespins.

1. Clip the crocodiles to the backs of kids' shirts. Tell kids to spread out randomly around the space.
2. Display the "John 1:34 Poster" (pack item 17) and read it together. Set the verse aside.
3. Set the timer for about two minutes. (You can adjust the time depending on the age and experience of your group.) On your signal, the kids work to find the first word and lead that person to stand in front of the group. They continue to find the words in order, trying to beat the timer.
4. Say the verse together again.
5. As time permits, remove the crocodiles, mix them, and place them on new volunteers to play again.

DAY 3

ENCOUNTER ON THE WATER

BIBLE STORY

Encounter on the Water (Matthew 14:22-33)

BIBLE VERSE

But these are written so that you may believe that Jesus is the Messiah, the Son of God, and that by believing you may have life in his name. *John 20:31*

But these are written, that ye might believe that Jesus is the Christ, the Son of God; and that believing ye might have life through his name. *John 20:31* (KJV)

TODAY'S POINT

Jesus proved He is God's Son.

LEADER DEVOTION

If you're hoping to see animals in the wild, it's easy to miss some great opportunities if you are in a hurry or fail to focus. But if you are alert and patient, what appears to be just another bush will reveal the flick of a tail or the twitch of an ear, and then you realize what has been there all along!

Today's passage is much the same. It may be a familiar story, but be alert! Ask the Holy Spirit to focus your heart to see a bit of something you may have missed before.

In verse 22, it says that Jesus "made" the disciples get into the boat. His command was going to put them right in the middle of a crisis. The disciples obeyed. Obedience sometimes puts us on course for rough seas. But rest assured, the One who made the sea is fully in control.

Some of the disciples were experienced fishermen and well aware of the surprise storms that could pop over the ridges that surrounded the Sea of Galilee, almost without warning. The disciples must have been tired. They had already crossed the sea earlier that day (v. 13), spent all day with Jesus while He taught, then helped feed five thousand plus people. Late into the night, rowing against the wind, they must have felt like they were going nowhere. I'm sure their tired brains thought their eyes were playing tricks on them when they saw movement on the water. Was it a ghost? Physically and emotionally exhausted, they cried out in fear.

Don't you love that "immediately" Jesus spoke to them? Jesus told them to have courage and not be afraid. "It is I" is literally translated "I Am." In God's amazing economy, He often packs tons of meaning into the most basic of statements. This allusion to Exodus 3:14 hinted again to the fact that "I and the Father are one" (John 10:30). Also interesting to note is Job 9:8 that hints of this very miracle.

Peter's response was to ask Jesus to command him to come walk on the water with Jesus. Peter was learning that power came from Jesus. Can you even imagine what those first steps were like for Peter? As a fisherman who had surely plunged into those depths many times, now Peter felt those waves solidly supporting his weight! Who could have kept from glancing around at this amazing phenomenon! Suddenly that sinking feeling returned, because he was indeed sinking! Peter cried out to the Lord for help, and Jesus reached out and caught hold of him. Jesus said, "You of little faith, why did you doubt?" Then together they climbed back into the boat ... and the wind stopped!

Have you ever experienced noise so loud you had to shout for the person next to you to be able to hear? When that noise stops suddenly, you almost hold your breath, the silence is so profound. Was that what the disciples experienced? Did they collectively hold their breath as what they had witnessed filled their senses? The next instant was a unanimous response of worship. Even though they had seen mind-blowing miracles earlier in the day, this encounter was an eye-opening experience and their heartfelt response was, "Truly You are the Son of God!"

PERSONAL FOCUS

- Read John 14:1 (today's bonus verse). How can this verse help you at this midpoint of VBS?

- Can you relate to the disciples' situation? Think back to a time when you were physically and emotionally drained. How has God spoken to you to restore your peace and courage?

TEACH THE BIBLE STUDY (30 MINUTES)

START IT PREP
- ❏ Animal crackers in a container

START IT (5 MINUTES)

1. Welcome kids back to the Watering Hole. Say: "Gathering at a watering hole, waiting to encounter different animals, you may hear different sounds. Let's play a sounds game."

2. Choose a volunteer to begin the game. Ask the volunteer to come in front of the group, reach into the container, and remove one of the animal crackers. He can glance at the animal but not show it to anyone else (except the leader). The child can make vocal sounds to lead the group to guess the animal. After the animal is guessed, choose another volunteer.

3. Say: "We have seen people have an encounter with Jesus in the temple and at the river. Today the encounter is on water. And this story also has something that makes sounds."

LEARN IT PREP
- ❏ Leader pack items 6, 18, 19
- ❏ Plastic hoop
- ❏ 4–6 large plastic cups or traffic cones

LEARN IT (12 MINUTES)

1. Say: "Watching animals is hard work. You must wait quietly and listen. You must be ready to take a snapshot of what you see quickly. We will practice listening and taking snapshots during the Bible story today."

2. Distribute copies of "Take a Snapshot" (pack item 19) and pencils. Tell kids to be prepared to quickly sketch snapshots during the story.

3. Open the Bible to Matthew 14:22-33. Pause where indicated and ask kids to sketch a snapshot.

ITEM 18

ENCOUNTER ON THE WATER

People followed Jesus everywhere He went. They wanted to hear Him teach about God.

After a long day of teaching near the Sea of Galilee, Jesus said goodbye to the crowds and told His small group of disciples to go ahead of Him in a boat. Then He went up on a mountain to pray.

(Sketch a snapshot of the boat.)

Late at night, the disciples' boat was far from shore. The winds began to blow and the water grew rough and choppy. The waves beat against their boat while the winds pushed harder and harder against them.

(Sketch a snapshot of the Sea of Galilee now.)

Very early in the morning, the disciples saw something coming toward them. It was Jesus walking on top of the water as if it were solid ground. As Jesus approached the disciples, they cried out in fear, "It's a ghost!"

Jesus called out to them, "Don't be afraid! It is I!"

Peter said, "Lord, if it is really You, let me walk on top of the water to You."

So Jesus said, "Come."

Peter climbed out of the boat and began walking on the water toward Jesus. How amazing! But then Peter began to notice how strong the wind was and got scared. He began to sink into the dark, turbulent water. He cried out, "Lord, save me!"

Jesus reached out and caught hold of Peter. Jesus asked Peter, "Why did you doubt Me? Is your faith really so small?"

(Sketch a snapshot of Jesus and Peter.)

Jesus and Peter got back into the boat, and immediately the wind stopped. Everything was calm. Not only could Jesus walk on water, His power could control the wind and the waves! The disciples worshiped Jesus and said, "It's true. You really are the Son of God."

Matthew 14:22-33

TIP
For a large group, create multiple "Meerkat Burrows."

4. Group kids into pairs. Tell partners to use their snapshots to recall the Bible story to one another. Display the "Day 3 Bible Story Picture" (pack item 18) and talk about the story as a group. Ask: "Why did the disciples say that Jesus really is the Son of God?"

5. Set the cups or cones on the floor in a circle and balance the plastic hoop on top of it. Choose 6–8 kids to stand around the hoop. Display the "John 20:31 Poster" (pack item 6). Tell kids they will play "Meerkat Burrow." As the group says the verse, a child will step into the hoop (burrow) without knocking it off the cups. A child should step into the burrow on each word the group says. When all meerkats are in the burrow, they step out for each word as the group continues the verse. Continue until the verse is complete. If the hoop is knocked down, all kids get out of the hoop and reset it. (You can choose to start the verse over again or continue where you left off.) As time permits, choose another group of kids and say the verse again.

TEACH THE BIBLE STUDY (30 MINUTES)

LIVE IT PREP
- ❏ Leader pack items 1, 2
- ❏ *VBS 2019 Field Guides: Grades 1–6* (1 per kid)
- ❏ Index cards with these references: *Exodus 14:14; Philippians 4:6-7; Proverbs 3:5-6; John 14:27*

LIVE IT (10 MINUTES)

1. Attach "Daily Snapshot 3" (pack item 2) to the "Watering Hole Banner" (pack item 1). Say: "In today's story we saw the wind and the waves become calm because of Jesus. The disciples knew that Jesus is God's Son. Jesus proved He is God's Son."

2. Say: "Because Jesus is God's Son, He can help people when they have difficult situations. He helped the disciples in their stormy trouble. He can help us, too."

3. Distribute cards and Bibles to four kids. Lead kids to find the references and read each of the verses aloud, one at a time. Talk about what the verse means and how those words could help someone in a difficult time.

4. Lead kids to turn to "Creature Comforts" (page 7) in the learner guide. Lead kids to match the verse references to the different "troubles."

5. Pray. Thank God for the Bible and for His Son who helps people in troubling times.

FINISH IT PREP
- ❏ Jesus chart from Day 1
- ❏ *VBS 2019 Field Guides: Grades 1–6* (1 per kid)
- ❏ *VBS 2019 Daily Verse Tags* (005809144)

FINISH IT (3 MINUTES)

1. Add today's point to the Jesus chart started on Day 1. Talk about other words or statements about Jesus that kids want to add. Look through the list to correct any statements based on today's story and point.

2. Say: "Calming the wind and waves was not the only way that Jesus proved He is God's Son. He did many other things that no person can do."

3. Point out "Up Close and Personal" (page 7) for Day 3 in the Field Guide. Challenge kids to read the Bible passage listed and find other Bible stories about Jesus that show things He did that prove He is God's Son.

4. If you have the Daily Verse Tags, distribute the Day 3 tags and encourage kids to look up the verse on their tag.

GATHER YOUR HERD
(Application Activity—10 minutes)

PREP

❑ Leader pack items 3, 10

❑ Masking tape

❑ *Optional:* Beanbag

❑ Create a 6-by-6 grid on the floor with masking tape.

1. Group the kids into two teams. Separate the "Animal Pictures" (pack item 3) by background color and give a group of cards to each team.

2. Alternate asking teams "Review Questions" (pack item 10). Use the questions for Days 1–3. When a team gets a question correct, they can place one of their animals in a grid square. (*Optional:* Toss the beanbag and place the animal where the beanbag lands.) A team wins when it gets a herd of four animals in a line.

3. Say: "Jesus proved He is God's Son." Repeat the point with kids. Say: "The Bible tells us that Jesus, God's Son, is the Savior. Our verse says that people have life by believing in Jesus. God sent Jesus to save people from their sins."

4. Talk about God's plan for Jesus. See "Sharing the Gospel with Kids" on the inside front cover.

BIRDWATCHING
(Application Activity—10 minutes)

PREP

❑ Leader pack item 20

1. Mix the pieces of the "Bird Puzzles" (pack item 20) and distribute the pieces to the kids.

2. Tell kids to work together to find the pieces that go together and assemble the bird puzzles.

3. Point out the words on the edges of the puzzles.

4. Read the statements. Say: "Jesus did things that no person could do. Jesus proved He is God's Son by the things that He did."

5. Distribute Bibles and help the kids find John 20:30-31. Read the verses. Say: "The words in the Bible are written so that we may know that Jesus is God's Son. Believing in Jesus, the Messiah, the Savior, saves people from their sins."

6. Look up verses and read about the miracles as time permits.

ANSWERS:

Jesus walked on the water. Matthew 14:22-33

Jesus healed a woman and a girl. Luke 8:40-56

Jesus fed more than 5,000 people. Luke 9:10-17

Jesus drove out an evil spirit. Luke 4:31-37

Jesus healed a deaf man. Mark 7:31-37

Jesus raised Lazarus from the dead. John 11:1-44

Jesus helped disciples catch fish. John 21:1-8

Jesus healed 10 people with leprosy. Luke 17:11-19

ITEM 20

ADDITIONAL ACTIVITY OPTIONS

DON'T GET STUNG
(Bible Skills Activity—10 minutes)

PREP

- ❏ Wide craft sticks
- ❏ Plastic cup
- ❏ Print the names of the Gospel books on the ends of 12 craft sticks. Print the name at one end of the stick rather than in the middle of the stick. Add the names of other Bible books (not Gospels) on the ends of 8 sticks. On the ends of 5 sticks, draw a simple figure of a bee. Mix the sticks together and place them, blank end up, in the cup.

1. Remind the kids that the Gospels are the books in the Bible that tell about Jesus' life. Say the four Gospels together: "Matthew, Mark, Luke, John."
2. Group kids into teams (or play individually with multiple sets of sticks). Explain that a child will pull a stick from the cup. She will read the book and tell whether or not it is a Gospel book. If she is correct, she keeps the stick; if she is incorrect then she places the stick back in the cup. If she gets "stung" (pulls out a bee stick), she must return all her sticks to the cup.
3. Continue alternating players for the time allowed. The player with the most sticks at the end of play wins.
4. Play for a few minutes. Reset and play a second time.
5. Pray, thanking God for the Bible that tells about His Son, Jesus.

SKY AND SEA REMINDERS
(Bonus Verse Activity—10 minutes)

PREP

- ❏ Leader pack item 21
- ❏ White construction paper
- ❏ Crayons
- ❏ Blue and black watercolors
- ❏ Water
- ❏ Paintbrushes

1. Display the "John 14:1 Poster" (pack item 21). Say the verse together.
2. Remind kids of the way that Jesus helped His disciples in today's Bible story. Comment that Jesus can help us when we have troubles, too. He is God's Son.
3. Tell kids they can make a reminder of the verse to help them remember that they can believe Jesus. Distribute paper. Tell kids to print the verse on the paper with the crayons. They can add sea animals or birds around their verses.
4. Lead kids to paint watercolor waves or stormy clouds over their verses. The watercolor will cover the paper but not cover the crayon. (For best results, use lighter colors of crayon.)
5. As kids finish their reminders, repeat the verse together.

DON'T LET YOUR **HEART BE TROUBLED.** BELIEVE IN GOD: **BELIEVE ALSO IN ME.**

JOHN 14:1

ITEM 21

DAY 4

ENCOUNTER AT THE TOMB

BIBLE STORY
Encounter at the Tomb (John 20:1-18)

BIBLE VERSE
But these are written so that you may believe that Jesus is the Messiah, the Son of God, and that by believing you may have life in his name. *John 20:31*

But these are written, that ye might believe that Jesus is the Christ, the Son of God; and that believing ye might have life through his name. *John 20:31 (KJV)*

TODAY'S POINT
Jesus rose from the dead.

LEADER DEVOTION

Do you look forward to that rare morning when you don't have to set an alarm or fly out of bed before the sun is even up? And, why is it that on those rare mornings, every bird in the neighborhood decides to put on a command performance in the tree right outside your bedroom? I love the sound of birds singing, but what is up with that early morning concerto? Did you know there is a name for it? It's called the "dawn chorus." There are several theories about this phenomenon, but in general, it seems to center around the male birds showing their power to stake a claim to a certain territory. It's sort of a "the night is over and I'm alive!" cry to the world.

On the third day after Jesus' crucifixion, most of His followers were feeling frightened and alone. Yet in the predawn darkness, the soft crunch of footsteps could be heard headed to the tomb where Jesus' body had been laid. The John passage only mentions Mary Magdalene, however other Gospels list other women and Mary's use of the word "we" in verse two indicates she was part of a group.

Considering that this is John's version of what happened, it's not surprising that his details involve those that impacted him directly. Mary Magdalene brought the news of the empty tomb to Peter and John, who raced off to see for themselves. John got to the tomb first and peered in. At this point the light of dawn was sufficient to see inside, and John described the linen burial cloths lying empty and made the special note that the head wrapping was folded up and placed separately from the rest. As John was noting this, Peter rushed past and ran straight into the tomb. John wrote that they "saw and believed" but "did not yet understand." Isn't this a great description of faith in Jesus? There is so much I believe and yet so much I don't understand.

From a Jewish perspective, John covered a couple of significant points. Under Jewish law, there must be two witnesses for evidence to be considered admissible. Peter and John both saw the empty tomb. The fact that they "did not yet understand" what the resurrection meant was further evidence that they didn't make up the story. Why would they make up facts about something that did not yet have significance to them? The neatly folded cloth also gave evidence to a careful sequence of events, not to grave robbers who would have more likely moved in haste.

After Peter and John left, Mary was still crying near the tomb. She stooped to look inside and saw two angels, one near the head of the burial shelf and one near the foot. The brief conversation is interesting. Rather than being startled that angels asked why she was crying, Mary was hyper focused on finding the body of her Lord. "They've taken away my Lord ... and I don't know where they've put Him."

As she turned, a man was standing there who also asked why she was crying. It's unclear why Mary did not immediately recognize Jesus. In some cases it appears that recognition only happens through divine revelation. Maybe she was crying so hard that everything was blurry. At any rate, Mary assumed the man was the gardener. (Who else would be working in the garden so early in the morning?)

Then Jesus spoke her name, "Mary." I'm sure to Mary's ears this was the sweetest "dawn chorus" ever heard. It was the Lord! The night was over and Jesus was alive!

PERSONAL FOCUS

- Today's bonus verse is John 14:6. Why is this verse important for today's session?
- Jesus appeared first to a woman and gave her the job of reporting His resurrection to the disciples. Why was this such a remarkable thing in that day and time?
- Peter and John knew what Jesus had told them about His coming death and resurrection, yet it was hard for them to believe. Why do you think people still have a hard time believing?

START IT (5 MINUTES)

1. Welcome kids back to the Watering Hole. Say: "Animals communicate with one another in the wild. They make different types of sounds and calls. They use gestures and move their bodies. Bees even dance to communicate with others at the hive."

2. Say: "We communicate in different ways, too. We talk and sing. We use movements with our bodies and hands. Some people who cannot hear use their hands to talk. They use sign language. Look at these signs and see if you can tell what animal name I am saying in sign language."

3. Use "Animal Sign Language" (pack item 22) and sign the different animal signs, one at a time. Encourage kids to guess the animal name. Lead them to sign the name with you after it is identified.

4. Review the points from Days 1–3 "Daily Snapshots" (pack item 2) posted on the "Watering Hole Banner" (pack item 1). Say: "Jesus is God's Son. He showed that He is God's Son by the things He said and did. Jesus knew why He had come. Today we will hear about why Jesus came and what happened."

LEARN IT (10 MINUTES)

1. Say: "All people need to learn about Jesus, God's Son. People who cannot hear need someone to tell them about Jesus. They can learn about Jesus through sign language. Let's learn the sign for Jesus."

2. Teach kids to make the sign for *Jesus*. (Touch middle finger of right hand to palm of open left hand; touch middle finger of left hand to palm of open right hand.)

3. Say: "As you listen to this story, make this sign every time you hear Jesus' name." Open the Bible to John 20:1-18. Tell the Bible story, pausing slightly after Jesus' name for kids to make the sign.

ENCOUNTER AT THE TOMB

Early in the morning, Mary Magdalene walked toward a hill outside Jerusalem, feeling very sad. Three days earlier, **Jesus** had died on a cross and been buried. Mary Magdalene was walking to the tomb where **Jesus** was buried. It was still dark as she approached the tomb, but she could see that the large stone at the entrance had been moved away.

Mary ran to find Peter and John, two of **Jesus**' disciples. "They've taken **Jesus** out of the tomb," she said. "We don't know where they have put Him!"

Peter and John ran to the tomb. John looked inside and saw the pieces of cloth that had been wrapped around **Jesus**' body lying there. Peter went into the tomb and saw that the cloth that had been around **Jesus**' head was folded up. But **Jesus** was gone. The tomb

START IT PREP
☐ Leader pack item 1, 2, 22

ITEM 22

LEARN IT PREP
☐ Leader pack items 6, 23

ITEM 23

was empty. Then John went into the tomb, saw, and believed. Up until that time, they had not understood that **Jesus** would be raised from the dead.

Peter and John went back to where they were staying, but Mary Magdalene stood near the tomb crying. Mary looked inside the tomb again and saw an amazing thing. Two angels were sitting where **Jesus**' body had been. They asked her, "Why are you crying?"

"Because someone has taken **Jesus** away, and I don't know where they've put Him," she said. Then Mary turned around and saw a man standing nearby. Mary did not recognize Him.

"Why are you crying? Who are you looking for?" He asked.

Mary thought the man was the gardener. So she said, "Sir, if you have taken **Jesus** away, please tell me where He is and I will go get Him."

But the man who stood before her was not the gardener. "Mary," the man said. Mary was shocked! She recognized that voice! It was **Jesus**! Mary turned around and said, "Teacher!"

Jesus sent Mary to tell the disciples this most amazing news. She ran back and told them, "I have seen **Jesus**!" He is alive!

John 20:1-18

4. Display the "Day 4 Bible Story Picture" (pack item 23). Ask: "What amazing thing happened?" *(Jesus was alive; He rose from the dead.)* Make the sign for Jesus again. Say: "This is the sign for Jesus because of what He did. Jesus died on a cross. In this sign, we touch our palms as reminders that Jesus was nailed to the cross. Jesus knew that the reason He came was to give His life to be our Savior. His death saves people from their sins."

5. Display "John 20:31 Poster" (pack item 6). Read the verse together. Say: "Our verse tells about this amazing encounter." Point out the last phrase of the verse (about having life in His name). Tell kids that they can create some signs to help them remember this verse. Identify some key words and tell kids to create their own signs for those words. (Or use these suggestions—*write:* pretend to write with a pencil; *believe:* point to forehead; *Jesus:* use sign already learned; *God:* point up; *life:* hold arms up) Repeat the verse, adding the signs as you say it.

LIVE IT (10 MINUTES)

1. Attach "Daily Snapshot 4" (pack item 2) to the "Watering Hole Banner" (pack item 1). Read the point and say it together. Remind kids that Jesus came to give His life to be our Savior.

2. Group the kids into five groups. Lead the groups to search around the room and "track down" one of the "Follow the Tracks" signs (pack item 25). Each group should take a sign back to the group area.

3. Use "Sharing the Gospel with Kids" on the inside cover to tell kids about these phrases. Tell the group with "God Rules" to hold up their track sign. Briefly tell (or read) what this means. Continue with the other track signs.

4. Display the three homemade signs. Tell kids about these three words, our response to the Holy Spirit to receive the gift God offers through Jesus.

5. Distribute the Field Guides and pencils. Lead kids to find "It Rocks!" (page 11). Tell them to draw something on one of the rocks to remember that Jesus rose from the dead.

FINISH IT (5 MINUTES)

1. Point out today's "Up Close and Personal" (page 11) in the Field Guide. Tell kids that Jesus did not just appear to Mary but to many other people as well. Challenge them to read in the Bible to find other people who saw Jesus after He rose from the dead.

2. Play and sing "What You're Made For" 🔊 (track 4).

3. If you have the Daily Verse Tags, distribute the Day 4 tags and encourage kids to look up the verse on their tag.

4. Pray. Thank God for sending Jesus to be our Savior. Thank Him that Jesus is still alive today.

LIVE IT PREP
- ❑ Leader pack items 1, 2, 25
- ❑ *VBS 2019 Field Guides: Grades 1–6* (1 per kid)
- ❑ Paper
- ❑ Place the "Follow the Tracks" (pack item 25) signs around the room. Make three signs: Admit, Believe, Confess.

FINISH IT PREP
- ❑ *VBS 2019 Field Guides: Grades 1–6* (1 per kid)
- ❑ *Music for Kids CD*
  - "What You're Made For" (track 4)
- ❑ *VBS 2019 Daily Verse Tags* (005809144)

MULTIMEDIA KEY
🔊 Audio
See page 1 for more information.

MONKEY MATCH
(Application Activity—10 minutes)

PREP

❏ Leader pack items 25, 26,

❏ Yarn

❏ Paper

❏ Scissors

1. Cut three lengths of yarn. Create a loop at the bottom of the *Admit* sign from "Monkey Match" (pack item 26) by taping the ends of a length of yarn to the bottom of the sign. Repeat with the *Believe* and *Confess* signs. Tape the three signs to a wall at child's eye level.

2. Review the phrases from "Follow the Tracks" (pack item 25). Use "Sharing the Gospel with Kids" from the inside front cover to talk about each of these phrases.

3. Point to the three words on the wall. Say that kids can look up verses in the Bible to learn more about these three words.

4. Distribute Bibles and the monkey shapes to pairs of kids. Lead the pairs to look up their verse reference and decide which word the verse applies to.

5. Lead pairs to hang their monkey shapes under the appropriate words. (The first monkey can hang from the yarn loop. The other monkeys can link together.)

6. Discuss Admit, Believe, and Confess and how the verses relate to these words.

7. Suggest kids print the three words and the verse references on paper and reread the verses at home.

ITEM 26

ANSWERS:
Admit: Acts 3:19; 1 John 1:9; Romans 3:23

Believe: Acts 16:31; Acts 4:12; Ephesians 2:8-9; John 14:6

Confess: Romans 10:9-10; Romans 10:13

FOUR HABITATS
(Application Activity—10 minutes)

PREP

❏ Leader pack items 10, 11

❏ *Music for Kids CD*

❏ Paper—Make four signs, each with one of the following words printed on it: *Rainforest, Tundra, Desert, Swamp*

❏ Tape the four signs in the four corners of the room or in four different areas of the space.

1. Play music from the *Music for Kids CD* 🔊. Lead kids to walk around the middle of the room. Stop the music unexpectedly. All kids should move to one of the four habitats.

2. Choose a habitat randomly. Ask the group at that habitat to answer a question. If the group responds correctly, start the music again for everyone to move. If the group responds incorrectly, they must step to the side and sit out one round of the game.

3. Ask questions about today's Bible story using "Review Questions" or "Discussion Questions" (pack items 10, 11). To extend the game, ask questions about Days 1–3.

4. Say John 20:31 together. Remind kids that Jesus came to be our Savior.

BOOK LEAPFROG

(Bible Skills Activity—10 minutes)

PREP

❑ Leader pack item 16

❑ Sort the "New Testament Cards" (pack item 16). Set aside the division names. Gather all the Gospel cards together. Gather the other Bible books into a second group.

1. Recall the four Gospel books with kids. Guide the kids to lay the Gospel cards in order on the floor or tape to a wall. *(Matthew, Mark, Luke, John, Matthew ....)*

2. Group kids into pairs. Lead the pairs to play leapfrog as they say the Gospel books. The first child kneels on the floor. The second child puts his hands on the first child's back and leaps over him as he says "Matthew." The first child leaps over the second while saying, "Mark." And so forth. The kids can use the cards as reminders.

3. Challenge the group to put all the New Testament books in order. (Remove repeats of the Gospel cards.)

4. Choose two volunteers to leapfrog while the group says the New Testament books. After a few books, switch volunteers and continue to say the Bible books in order.

5. Comment that the whole Bible tells about God's plan to save people from sin.

VERSE COMPASS

(Bonus Verse Activity—10 minutes)

PREP

❑ Leader pack item 24

❑ Paper plates (2 per child)

❑ Scissors

❑ Brads (one per child)

1. Tell kids that traveling through different areas looking for animals can be challenging. People often use a compass or GPS to find their way.

2. Display the "John 14:6 Poster" (pack item 24) and read the verse. Say: "Jesus told us that to find the way to God, people had to know about Him. Jesus is the only way to God."

3. Tell kids they can make a "compass" of this Bible verse. Distribute two plates to each child.

4. Tell kids to cut the rim off of one of their plates. On the cut plate, they can draw an arrow pointing to the plate's edge. They can draw a picture about today's Bible story or other designs about Jesus on the cut plate.

5. Help kids print the verse around the rim of the uncut plate. Show kids how to use a brad to punch a hole in the middle of each of their plates. Then place the cut plate on top of the uncut one and attach them together with the brad.

6. Spin one of the verse compasses, showing how the arrow points to the words of the verse. Say the verse together as kids turn their compasses.

7. Pray, thanking God for sending Jesus to be the Savior, the way to Him.

DAY 5

ENCOUNTER ON THE ROAD

BIBLE STORY
Encounter on the Road (Luke 24:13-35)

BIBLE VERSE
But these are written so that you may believe that Jesus is the Messiah, the Son of God, and that by believing you may have life in his name. *John 20:31*

But these are written, that ye might believe that Jesus is the Christ, the Son of God; and that believing ye might have life through his name. *John 20:31* (KJV)

TODAY'S POINT
The Bible was written so I can believe.

LEADER DEVOTION

Recently I was chatting with a friend who loves to hike. (I only hike occasionally when coerced by my family.) He is also aware of my abject phobia of a certain "legless" creature. "You know," he said, "they blend so well with their surroundings, I wonder how many times we've all walked right by them without seeing them." Yikes! I immediately looked around and we were in a concrete office building six floors up!

Sometimes we don't see things because we aren't looking and sometimes we don't see them because we don't expect them to be there. And, in God's own plan and blessing, sometimes we are prevented from seeing ... until just the right time.

On the day of Jesus' resurrection two of His followers were making the approximately 7-mile trek from Jerusalem back to their home in Emmaus. We know the name of one of the men, Cleopas (who some Bible scholars think may have been the husband of one of the women at the foot of the cross— John 19:25).

The men were talking about the events of the last few days and the reports from the women and the disciples about Jesus' resurrection. A man fell into step with them and joined their conversation. My mind races with questions. Why these two guys? They weren't part of the inner circle. Why the mysterious "so what's up guys" approach? Isn't this the time for an encore of the heavenly host who announced His birth? God's choices and timing are amazing and mind-boggling. Two ordinary guys were chosen by God to hear the full explanation of the gospel from Genesis to this true moment of revelation. Cleopas and his friend were shocked that their traveling partner seemed unaware of the mind-blowing events of the past few days in Jerusalem. And then this man began to speak. He explained how Scripture foretold everything that had happened. He talked about how the Messiah had to come and why He had to suffer.

The trio arrived in Emmaus near day's end and the two travelers invited their new friend to stay for the evening meal. As they prepared to eat, Jesus broke the bread and blessed it. At that moment Jesus' identity was revealed. The men were astounded ... and Jesus disappeared. My imagination is fired up again! Did they jump up from the table too excited to eat and race back to Jerusalem? Did they grab a hunk of that precious blessed and broken bread to sustain them for that 7-mile sprint back to Jerusalem? Either way, an unexpected face-to-face encounter with Jesus was not an experience to keep to themselves. The other disciples had to know!

Knowing Jesus is life-changing. Experiencing His presence is something that has to be shared.

PERSONAL FOCUS

- Read Romans 10:17 (today's bonus verse). Why is the message about Jesus Christ so important?
- Think about a time when you were most aware of Jesus in your life. How would you describe it to someone?
- In the busy-ness of VBS, it's easy to lose the urgency of telling others about Him. Pray that God would make clear those moments when you can share the gospel with someone.

START IT PREP
- ❏ Leader pack items 1, 2
- ❏ *Music for Kids CD*

START IT (5 MINUTES)

1. Welcome kids as they arrive. Play music and encourage them to move around like elephants. Tell kids that when the music stops, you are taking a snapshot so they must freeze.

2. Stop the music unexpectedly and say: "Click!" Kids freeze. Before you start the music again, say: "Now you are turtles." Start the music. After a minute, stop and say: "Click!" Kids freeze.

3. Change animals again and start the music again. Play for several rounds.

4. Call kids to gather and sit near the "Watering Hole Banner" (pack item 1). Read each of the "Daily Snapshots" for Days 1–4 (pack item 2). Say: "We have learned a lot about Jesus. How do we know these things? Where do we encounter them?" *(the Bible)* Attach "Daily Snapshot 5" to the banner. Read today's Point.

LEARN IT PREP
- ❏ Leader pack items 7, 8 or 9, 10, 11, 27, 28
- ❏ *Music for Kids CD*
  - "What God Has Done" (track 3)
- ❏ Highlighters or markers (one per child)
- ❏ Bag
- ❏ Scissors
- ❏ Cut the verse strips apart, with 1–2 words on each piece. Put the pieces in a bag.

LEARN IT (12 MINUTES)

1. Say: "Today we will hear a Bible story in which someone talked about the Scriptures. What does the word Scriptures mean?" *(the Bible)*

2. Distribute copies of "Track the Bible Story" (pack item 28) and highlighters. Say: "Listen for these words in the Bible story. Not all these words are in the story. Highlight a word when you hear it used."

3. Open the Bible to Luke 24:13-35. Display the "Day 5 Bible Story Picture" (pack item 27). Tell the Bible story, making sure to include the bolded words for kids to highlight.

ITEM 27

ENCOUNTER ON THE ROAD

On the day that **Jesus** rose from the dead, two men were walking toward the village of Emmaus. As they walked, they talked about everything that had happened during the last week. While they talked, Jesus joined them, but they did not recognize Him.

Jesus asked them, "What are you talking about?"

The two men stopped walking and looked at each other with **sadness**. One of the men, Cleopas, answered, "Are you the only person in all of Jerusalem who doesn't know what has happened?"

"What happened?" Jesus asked.

So the men began to talk about everything that had happened to Jesus in the last week. They explained that Jesus was a great Prophet (someone who delivers God's message to people) who acted and spoke with great power. They explained how Jesus was put on trial and crucified.

"We had hoped He was the **Messiah** God promised to send," they said, "but He's been dead for three days now. This morning, some women went to His tomb and saw angels who told them that Jesus is alive again. Some of our friends went to the tomb, and they also saw that it was empty."

Jesus asked, "Don't you remember what the **prophets** wrote? They said all of these things would have to happen to the Messiah." Then Jesus began to quote from the Old Testament **Scriptures**, and He explained to the men how those Scriptures prove that Jesus is who He says He is.

When they got to the village of Emmaus, the men invited Jesus to stay with them. As they sat at the dinner table together, Jesus took some **bread**, thanked God for it, and tore it into pieces. He gave the pieces to the men. At that moment, the men recognized Him. They knew He was Jesus. Then, Jesus disappeared from their sight.

The men thought back to their walk that day. They said, "Didn't we feel excited when Jesus explained to us what the Scriptures mean? It was like our hearts were on fire!" They got up and immediately went back to Jerusalem. They found Jesus' eleven **disciples** and others who had gathered with them. They told them what had happened on the road and how they recognized Jesus when He had broken the bread. The disciples were amazed. What an amazing encounter with Jesus!

Luke 24:13-35

MULTIMEDIA KEY
🔊 Audio
See page 1 for more information.

4. Tell kids to look at their highlighted words. Ask: "What shape do you see? *(J)* Yes, J as in Jesus. The men did not recognize Jesus at first. But they learned about what the Scriptures, the Bible, says about the Messiah. They realized that Jesus is the Messiah."

5. Talk about the "Day 5 Bible Story Picture" (pack item 27). Use the "Review Questions" and "Discussion Questions" (pack items 10–11) to talk more about the Bible story.

6. Play "What God Has Done" 🔊 (track 3). Pass the bag of verse words around the group. Stop the music and ask the child holding the bag to remove a word. She can tape the word to the "Verse Map" (pack item 7). Start the music again. After several words are on the map, tell the child holding the bag that he can either remove another word or rearrange words on the map to be in the correct order. Continue until the verse is assembled.

7. Read the verse together. Pray, thanking God for the Bible that helps us know about Jesus and what He did to save us.

TEACH THE BIBLE STUDY (30 MINUTES)

LIVE IT PREP
- ❏ *VBS 2019 Field Guides: Grades 1–6* (1 per kid)
- ❏ Homemade Jesus chart

LIVE IT (9 MINUTES)

1. Say today's Point together. Say: "Let's think about what you know or have learned about Jesus." Review the chart about Jesus you started on Day 1. Adjust any statements as needed. Add any others needed. (Make sure "Jesus is the Savior" is on the chart.)

2. Distribute the Field Guides. Guide kids to find "Describe Your Habit-at" (page 13). Tell kids to look at the pictures on the page. Then work with kids around them to identify each of the places.

3. Say: "The men encountered Jesus on the road in today's Bible story. You can encounter Jesus in these places. You can help others encounter Jesus in these places. How can you share about Jesus with others?" Encourage kids to name ways they could share about Jesus.

4. Lead kids to pray and ask God to help them tell about Jesus in the different places they go. Call on volunteers to pray. Allow as many to pray as choose to do so. Ask an adult to close the prayer time.

FINISH IT PREP
- ❏ Leader pack item 2
- ❏ *VBS 2019 Field Guides: Grades 1–6* (1 per kid)
- ❏ *VBS 2019 Daily Verse Tags* (005809144)

FINISH IT (4 MINUTES)

1. Call attention to "Daily Snapshot 5" (pack item 2). Repeat today's Point together.

2. Say: "The words in the Bible help us know about Jesus and believe in Him. The Bible also helps us learn and grow when we are Christians."

3. Lead kids to find today's "Up Close and Personal" (page 13) in the Field Guide. Challenge kids to read the Bible at home next week. Turn to the reading pages in the Field Guide (pages 14–16). Say: "This guide can help you get started reading the Bible at home."

4. If you have the Daily Verse Tags, distribute the Day 5 tags and encourage kids to look up the verse on their tag.

5. Pray, thanking God that we can read the Bible and learn more about Him.

6. Tell kids you are glad they came to In the Wild™!

SNAPSHOT JOURNAL

(Application Activity—10 minutes)

PREP

❑ Leader pack item 2

❑ Paper

❑ Stapler and staples

❑ Other art supplies

1. Display and read the "Daily Snapshots" (pack item 2). Say: "We can make a snapshot journal of what we have learned at VBS."

2. Invite kids to make journals. They can print the Points on pieces of paper, one per page. They can draw pictures or symbols for each story. If a child struggles with what to draw, suggest she could draw the five places where people encountered Jesus—temple, river, boat on the lake, tomb, and road.

3. Tell kids they could use their snapshot journals to tell others what they have learned about Jesus.

4. Say John 20:31 together. Kids may want to include the verse in their journals.

5. Help kids stack their pages together and staple along one side to bind their journals.

WORDSSS AND ACTIONSSS CHART

(Application Activity—10 minutes)

PREP

❑ Leader pack item 15, 29

❑ Self-stick notes

❑ Gel pens

❑ On separate self-stick notes, print *Words* and *Actions*; place these at the tops of the columns on the "Anaconda Chart" (pack item 15). Display the chart.

1. Say the Point. Tell kids that reading in the Bible helps us know what Jesus said and did.

2. Distribute the Bibles and "Verses About Jesus" (pack item 29). Lead kids to work alone or in pairs to read the verses about Jesus. They can write down something Jesus said or did on self-stick notes. (Assign verses to kids so all verses are read and reviewed. You can assign the same verse to more than one child or pair.)

3. After a few minutes, call the group back together. Lead kids to tell what they read/noted. They can place their notes in the appropriate column on the chart.

4. Say: "Learning what Jesus said and did helps lead people to believe in Him. The Bible is how people learn that Jesus is the Savior."

MATTHEW 3:13-16	MARK 10:14-15
MARK 8:22-26	JOHN 14:6
MATTHEW 14:25	LUKE 18:27
JOHN 13:3-5	JOHN 3:16
LUKE 6:27	MARK 9:35

ITEM 29

ADDITIONAL ACTIVITY OPTIONS

GROUP 'EM UP
(Bible Skills Activity—10 minutes)

PREP

❏ Leader pack item 16

❏ Set aside the cards with the divisions from "New Testament Cards" (pack item 16). Hide the Bible books around the room.

1. Tell kids that groups of animals sometimes have different names. Give these examples: flock of sheep; herd of deer; pack of dogs; army of caterpillars; pod of dolphins; leap of leopards; pride of lions; crash of rhinoceroses; zeal of zebras.

2. Say: "We have a name for groups of Bible books, too. That group is called a division. There are five divisions in the New Testament." Display the division cards.

3. Say that Bible books are placed or hidden around the room. Kids will need to go and gather those cards. On your signal, kids can gather the cards and bring them back.

4. Help kids sort the books into divisions. They should know the Gospels so find those first and place them under the Gospels card.

5. Say: "There is one book of History. It tells about the early church, after Jesus returned to heaven. That book is after the Gospels." *(Acts)*

6. Say: "There is one book of Prophecy. It tells what will happen when Jesus returns to earth. It's the last book of the New Testament, the last book of the Bible." *(Revelation)*

7. Help kids sort the remaining books into the last two groups.

8. As time permits, mix the cards and sort the books again.

ANSWERS:
Gospels: Matthew, Mark, Luke, John

History: Acts

Paul's Letters: Romans, 1 Corinthians, 2 Corinthians, Galatians, Ephesians, Philippians, Colossians, 1 Thessalonians, 2 Thessalonians, 1 Timothy, 2 Timothy, Titus, Philemon

General Letters: Hebrews, James, 1 Peter, 2 Peter, 1 John, 2 John, 3 John, Jude

Prophecy: Revelation

AVOID THE SCAT
(Bonus Verse Activity—10 minutes)

PREP

❏ Leader pack item 30

❏ Paper

❏ Print the words of the Day 5 bonus verse on paper, one or two words per page. Also print these words on pieces of paper, one per page: *Emmaus, road, zebra, Peter, however, badger, encounter.* Create 20 different word pages. Mix the words and arrange them in a 4-by-5 grid on the floor. (Tape the paper down if you choose.)

1. Display the "Romans 10:17 Poster" (pack item 30) and read it together.

2. Say: "Hearing the message of the Bible, the good news about Jesus that God has given us in His Word, is how people believe. Faith comes through hearing the Bible. That's why we want to read it and memorize verses, so we can know more about God and His plan for us through Jesus."

3. Call attention to the word grid on the floor. Tell kids that they will step on the words of the verse in order. Comment that some words on the floor are not in the verse.

4. Say: "When someone is out exploring and looking for animals, he tries to avoid stepping in an animal's scat, or waste that the animal leaves when it goes to the bathroom. You want to avoid the scat—the words that do not belong in the verse."

5. Choose a volunteer to stand on the first word of the verse. Lead that child to step on the next words in order. Tell the group to say the words as the child steps on them. The group can help him step through the verse, avoiding the words that don't belong (scat).

6. If he steps on an incorrect word, he leaves the grid and another child takes a turn.

7. Pray and thank God for the Bible that helps us believe. Say the Point.

SUPPLIES

EVERYDAY SUPPLIES

(These items, needed every day in VBS, are only listed here and do not appear in each day's specific supply listing.)

- ❏ Bibles
- ❏ *VBS 2019 Field Guide: Grades 1–6* (005805594, one per kid)
- ❏ *VBS 2019 Grades 1–2 Bible Study Leader Pack* (005804846), including the *Music for Kids CD* found in the pack
- ❏ CD player
- ❏ Pencils and markers
- ❏ Tape

DAY 1

- ❏ Large piece of paper
- ❏ **Growth Chart** *(Application Activity)*
  - No additional supplies needed
- ❏ **Animal Camouflage** *(Application Activity)*
  - Paper
  - Crayons
- ❏ **Tiger Tails** *(Bible Skills Activity)*
  - Wide craft sticks
  - Orange markers
  - Narrow black ribbon or black paper
  - Scissors
  - Glue
- ❏ **Rabbit Run** *(Bonus Verse Activity)*
  - Self-stick notes or note cards (one color per team)

DAY 2

- ❏ Self-stick notes
- ❏ Animal stickers
- ❏ **Animal Tags** *(Application Activity)*
  - Circle key tags with split rings
  - Scissors
  - Colored cardstock
  - Glue
  - Gel pens
- ❏ **Picture This** *(Application Activity)*
  - Photograph of the baptistry or place where people are baptized in your church
- ❏ **Flipper Slap** *(Bible Skills Activity)*
  - 2 large gray oven mitts
- ❏ **Croc Attack** *(Bonus Verse Activity)*
  - Clothespins (green if available)
  - Timer

DAY 3

- ❏ Animal crackers in a container
- ❏ Plastic hoop
- ❏ 4–6 large plastic cups or traffic cones
- ❏ Index cards
- ❏ **Gather Your Herd** *(Application Activity)*
  - Masking tape
  - *Optional:* Beanbag
- ❏ **Birdwatching** *(Application Activity)*
  - No additional supplies needed
- ❏ **Don't Get Stung** *(Bible Skills Activity)*
  - Wide craft sticks
  - Plastic cup
- ❏ **Sky and Sea Reminders** *(Bonus Verse Activity)*
  - White construction paper
  - Crayons
  - Blue and black watercolors
  - Water
  - Paintbrushes

DAY 4

- ❏ Paper
- ❏ **Monkey Match** *(Application Activity)*
  - Yarn
  - Paper
  - Scissors
- ❏ **Four Habitats** *(Application Activity)*
  - Paper
- ❏ **Book Leapfrog** *(Bible Skills Activity)*
  - No additional supplies needed
- ❏ **Verse Compass** *(Bonus Verse Activity)*
  - Paper plates
  - Scissors
  - Brads

DAY 5

- ❏ Highlighters or markers
- ❏ Bag
- ❏ Scissors
- ❏ **Snapshot Journal** *(Application Activity)*
  - Paper
  - Stapler and staples
  - Other art supplies

- ❏ **Wordsss and Actionssss Chart** *(Application Activity)*
  - Self-stick notes
  - Gel pens
- ❏ **Group 'em Up** *(Bible Skills Activity)*
  - No additional supplies needed
- ❏ **Avoid the Scat** *(Bonus Verse Activity)*
  - Paper